WIPE THE MIRROR

ISAAC MIZRAKI

POEMS

GORHAM HOUSE PRESS

Contents

Wipe the Mirror
Isaac Mizraki Poems
Copyright © 2020 Isaac Mizraki. All rights reserved.
⟲ @wipethemirror

ISBN: 978-1-7346155-0-0
Published by Gorham House Press

Publication Design - Brady Book Design
www.bradybookdesign.com

Illustrations by Irma Soriano
⟲ @irmasuniverse

Printed in San Francisco.

to my sister Ginette
for always being there
and
to my mother Mathilde Gordon
for teaching me life's lessons

Earth

Voices

Open your eyes
and listen to those
little voices
they're asking the right
questions

Wipe the mirror

In search of purpose
start first
with knowing you
then stay true
to your best friend
proudly aware of actions
where goodness prevails
and values never shift with favor
beliefs less resolute in conviction
for sadly
life's journey can leave bruises
even when calmly tacking
let alone fighting raging storms
take care when punching back
for you may just lose
fondness for your own company
your living legacy in jeopardy
as unknowingly
the compass needle can shift
so
when the misted mirror
wonders who you are
don't lose your best friend
this is the time
disconnect to reconnect
turn yourself in
find the better you
transparent in authenticity
trusting in spirit
for all to see
with nothing to hide
from you

FIND FATHER

What is down below
in a hidden geophysical laboratory
mixing elements
conducting
chemical experiments
an endless cacophony
of pre-life reactions
soup cooking
a timeless endeavor
a baptism of conversion
making simple complex
inorganic organic
amino acids proteins
single molecules armies
of self-assembling organic molecules
a biological revolution in time
stumbling upon ribonucleic acid
that landscape design architect
molecular evolution into cells
delivered finally
with a huff and a puff
protectively midwifed in water
through hydrothermal vents
Mother Earth's vagina
now searching for the father

HEY YOU

Hey you
what's your story
start anywhere
I've got time
that's hard you say
start where
maybe with something you lost
that made you happy or sad
I'm listening
let the words flow like tears
that swell
then run
down the face of your life
I am that stranger
you'll never meet again
this is the funeral you never had
so close your eyes
allow the grief
to enter your soul
mourning nights shall wane
days again shine bright
see how memory
will mysteriously replace pain
with happiness and gratitude
for what you once had
more
for what you have today

AERO ON MONTANA

I won
that crazy debate
and went out
the parking was easy
the line fast
and joining the frenzied
mass of coke addicts
gave me a high
I couldn't understand
but it swept me in
past all those
featureless faces
till I found my own
glass cocoon
and settled in
ready for my two-hour hibernation
to a place
my friends said I should go
but as my brain
became a celluloid blob
a distant voice
called my name
freezing the cut
to the voice behind me
hi
that's a face from
the Miracle Shop
are you alone

Alone
aLone
alOne
aloNe
alonE
aLone
aLOne
ALONE
my head wanted to burst
with the reverberating peals
stop
and as I say
yes
a white spotlight
suddenly pinpointed me
blinded me
then flashed off
comforted by darkness
I slid down lower
only to hear that voice
again
it's wonderful
that you go out on your own
sitting in a shattered cocoon
that voice that
lost the debate
returns
told you to
rent a video

THE TEA HOUSE

Not ready for that class
forget what they said
no red light for me
my shortcut to life lessons
long night classes
trusting would-be friends
finding teachers that mostly couldn't
at that corner tea house
with different bags of pure magic
sipped eagerly from porcelain
what tribe demands such a price
a soul for an empty smile
what spell captured me in
blindly loving empty air
searching for confidence
that desperate quest
for acceptance by others
running away from me
a mystery to be solved
in a false paradise
till in one class
a lesson

no "should" must ever dictate
in that moment
a revelation of true self
a part of me gifted back to me
strength regained
denial removed
knowing too
never to misplace
my protective coat
against the dragons of deceit
uncovering that search
for a simple approval
that came only from me
and on that sunny San Francisco day
I walked home

STILLNESS

Moments of contact
spiraling in search
of truth
responding in frenetic
Morse code
too quiet to decipher
unintelligible
in the noisy reality
of interference
coming from everywhere
so
you don't really know
and maybe you're wrong
hearing the message
you wanted to hear
finally
in silence
you hear
those old words again
you see
what you never
saw then

Try this shoe

One day I discovered
my well-worn camouflage
only hid me from myself
unknowingly naked
in plain sight
failed protection
from arrows piercing the heart
from unlocking eyes paralyzing my voice
intelligent ignorance
a veil of self-imposed detachment
a survivor's secret handshake
uniting teams of appearances
where unknown hands lock in line
with voices in chorus
singing a public plea
to try on this shoe
on your beautiful tree-lined road
pass by my ankle-twisting
pot-holed street
please
no sympathy
just accept all of me
as I do all of you
with all of your
invisible sensitivities
should you choose to share them

Socks

So ready for the world
with no practice
matched souls
perfectly paired
freshly unwrapped team
striding streets
completely in tandem
yet beware
let not the air be pungent with
sweat
nor speak of things most foul
remember rebirth arrives
with every submersion
till the expected return
of the dreaded
single sock
magical disappearing act
once happy socks
suddenly lost
alone
neglected in drawers
sulking in shadows
barely touched
orphaned
till perchance
confused hands
create a new pair
who looks anyway
but see
the unmatched
can stride as a team
the single
walk alone

DELIVERANCE

When I hear the
sea pounding the rocks
I think of us
bobbing around
with no anchor
dangerously drawn
to the frothing saliva
of some underground
demon intent
on destruction
then casually watch
as we each try to save ourselves
grappling slippery rocks
that slide you
back into the jaws
hoping to avoid
crunching contact
with jagged teeth

GIVE A SUNRISE

What's your give
your contribution
to make the world a better place
money
time
love
music
art
education
food
shelter
wellness
thank you for caring
how about a warm hug
or a smile only for you
actually
the very best gift I have
is 100% of me
right now
my ears and eyes
a direct pathway to my heart
listening
absorbing
connecting
feeling
no brain interference

criticizing
judging
rejecting
arguing
debating
questioning
but that's critical thinking
you say
fine
stop the critical back talk
it's just advice
you say
to help
that's my give
really
maybe stop lecturing
and try being there
sharing the space
now that's a true give
an offering
like a beautiful sunrise

Life

Rose in bloom

Who can miss
that beautiful bouquet
perfectly matched
bringing color to dull space
such modest elegance
attracting admiring glances
yet always that true listener
with full ears
twinkling eyes
and surely too
that soft chuckle
hardly distracted in easy banter
sharing sincere space
a graceful gift from the heart
with a compassionate voice
for the concerns of all
well
maybe not all
oh come on John
really

SPINNER

Haunted and hounded
by family webs
of complexes
the organizer has planned
his escape
only to be entangled
in his success
and remain
a prisoner
in the same web
waiting to be devoured
in the same way
he devoured
others

ESCAPE

The house is full
of empty rooms
and hollow laughter
fills the ears of
a new family
and the little people
trying to survive
the branding
of that hot iron
across their soul
cry silently under
their all-powerful
God-given protection
convincing them
hoping then
believing that
there will be
a way out

EVERYDAY

Sunrise presents
its daily gift
another chance
make it different
from yesterday

sunsets hypnotize
and bodies
enveloped in color
invisibly carried
to a perfect end

No return

In the prison of morality
surrounded by invisible walls
we see rainbow-colored people outside
beckoning us to break out
from our self-made prisons
but when you discover
there never was a door
and walk out
remember
that door is invisible
for when you discover
there never was a rainbow
you'll be doomed
to an eternal search
for the door

Shai

In whatever traveled land
there may be a flower
forever in bloom
whose smiling petals
warmly welcome all
strangers alike
happy to bring joy
to all around
creatively challenging the moment
yet always composed in grace
the perfect listener
present in the now
for you

A SECOND'S FATE

Galaxies created
lives changed
souls saved
hearts lost
mortal eternity in a second
what lottery decides
not another second
painfully destroying dreams
for others
joyfully creating faith
but what answer for saving sanity
only escape in time lost
as tearful questions
blindly torment
and weary search parties
may never find
that ghostly body
invisible
in a desert sandstorm
a winter fog
existing in breathless darkness
as blank eyes
unknowingly await
rebirth
another second's fate

BORN AGAIN

Isn't it a shame to die
just when you've learnt to live
it's been a while
since I ditched that day
no one said
there wasn't a make-up class
and no cliff notes
so I tried all those classes
where I became a paying spectator
of my own life
with a great seat
of course
but trash those 3D glasses
they don't work
and the program's about you
not me
so I walked out
the ticket seller smiled
and nodded knowingly
he could have been me
maybe he was
the gatekeeper to the holy revelation
where everybody agrees to see
what's not there
and live happily ever after

but not if you blink
mistakenly breaking the spell
the questions remain
multiplying till brain fallout
leaves you with one
that one takes time
to see
the answer doesn't help
so now I need
a little more time
put my exit on hold
let me dance with life tonight
now that
I know the steps

GONE

This morning
I met a stranger
in my bed
same face
different words
have we met
somewhere before

UNWELCOME

I was
a pot-bellied
husband
drinking beer at the barbecue
joking with the guys
about the gals
and then I was
not part of
that club

REALITY

Cottage cheese and apple
with hiking and biking
is going to keep
you alive
a little longer
does anyone
really care
what's so important
about a particle
of cosmic dust
in the galaxy
of our universe

Angels

When the promise of the dream
was broken
there were
no days
for memories of rainbow times
too painful to touch
thanks for amnesia
God's
drug free
space age
turn on
rebirth at forty
mom and sis
there
suddenly
where
have they been
where
was I
they carried me out
of that cotton wool coffin

LITTLE FINGERS

Days can shine
again
close your hand
my little loved ones
and see your
power to do
and when you slowly open your
fingers
see the flowers in your hand
that is your power to think
take each day as a new visit
to the stars
put space between
your days
follow the torch in your hand
you will discover
life's magic
again

PATHS

Life is like our hikes
you're alone but not
you see what no one can
your tread can be rocky or
smooth
only you decide where to go
select your path carefully
for they are truly not restricted
duty and destiny
run parallel
fear not
if other paths cross
so be it
be true

WOODSTOCK

When murder survives
the lives
it strives
to kill
and hate continues
the path
of wrath it desires
and love exalts
the challenge
it cannot manage
and time tortures
the years
it fears to destroy
then tell the people they are
not people
and tell the children they are
not children
and tell me I am
not me
for then life's life is dead
and living a dead life is
not living
for not living
is not giving
and not giving
is not loving
and not loving

is not living
so die
lift yourself onto another point
like going out on a joint
in places
where faces
are traces of nothingness
and eyes
like skies
are lies of emptiness
and ears
like tears
are fears of darkness
so blow rings
like things
on wings
with your lips
the zips
to free trips for all

MY RAINBOW

Inside of me
there is
a coat of pain
who put
it there
that black stripe
on my rainbow

Recompass

Stick to your guns
stay the course
never quit
the best advice
maybe not
think a little more
listen a lot more
for there is no
I know it all
one day friends may say
I told you so
you just never listened
know when confidence
becomes arrogance
haughty spirit
invites destruction
so
don't close your mind
there are choices
let your mind wander
in green forests
along winding streams
explore the different paths
resilience
the better lesson
recompass
the way forward

Place

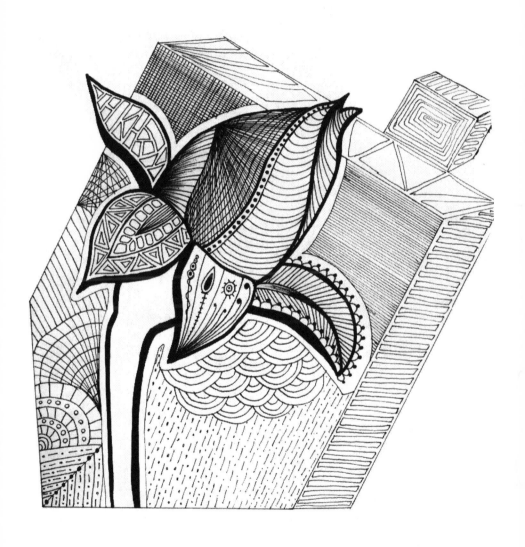

ARCTICA

On Mother Earth
there is a place
that after a fiery death
in poetic harmony
there is rebirth
costumed in unthemselves
followers afar
in sworn testimony
join the annual migration
to give and grow
to touch and receive
the very best of each
be sure to snorkel
the beautiful gray seas
to behold such creatures
whose shapes amaze
with colors unknown
in every corner
sudden surprises
all with primal voices that speak
to the beat of the heart

in deep
between the temple and the pyramid
there is a space with no time
where the sea gently whispers its message
let the warmth of memories carry you
as cold waters invigorate
with the possibilities of tomorrow
gliding in procession
fish blink rainbow hellos
in an unchoreographed dance of life
so farewell
be well
do good
with my De Mentha Camp mojito in hand
I receive
the gift of today

SANTA BARBARA

Boats dozing
in the goodnight sun
paint shadows in
gray and pink
across bikes
racing past
whispering lovers
and wheels on feet
chasing dogs
on leashes
ignore
the forgotten faces
whose eyes
hear the words
we speak
and ears
make the pictures
we see
and whose heart
tells them
they are in
the sanctuary
of happiness

NOWHERE

Sax in the night
ice in the glass
smoke in the air
three regulars
with the same story
does it ever change
not the end
the circle must break
and strangers
soon become lovers
bonded by untold secrets
that can only lead to
nowhere
a place in between
here and there
where
you can become who you wish
and babies don't cry
because they're left here
dare we leave
nowhere

BAR NONE

It's okay
to live in all four seasons
embrace those feelings
sense every change
no need to seek California sunburn
that terminal happiness
of stale air in false light
let the fall leaves inspire
your heart match the colors
in darkening days
walk backwards
to startle your mind
and see the day as others do
never alone in your loneliness
for remember
if ever black clouds appear
breathe deep
rub your hands
take a walk to anywhere
that hidden place
where
like me

you may just wander
into your own
OK Corral
discovering new strangers
around golden embers
whose enveloping smiles
wrapped in red ribbon hugs
will soon become
a beautiful gift of caring
even the chance
of touching a shooting star
see
you are okay
no
you are perfect
well
almost

ENCHANTED STAR

Across green plains and parched
mountains
under cool nights touched by
stars
my caravanserai brought me
to waters so blue the sky cried
in Karşıyaka with beauty
abounding
no man ever good enough
to Ankara where flowers bloom
everyman quite good enough
why eyes sincere
words so bright
would shed her robe to puffed
air
know well your worth
far deeper than touch
in your butterfly time
be ready
when the moon shall broadly
smile upon you
sending a favored star
to pierce your heart
flutter your wings
and breathe deep
your eternal gift in mortal days
too soon shall pass

MAUI

It's the place
where friendly palms
wave at
jogging clouds
where the sun
lazily walks over the
blue
around
green
a timeless zone
where hanging out
is in
sad stories
are out
and the search
is useless
it's the place
where the answer
finds you

SANTA MONICA

Ocean
at Santa Monica
dream factory
to the world
on tap for me
like a pint
at the pub
instant fun
hides
the real stuff
below
but will
the dreams
stop
after cleaning
up the mess

OKLAHOMA

I have never been
to Oklahoma
sometimes
I dream of it
seeing those
friendly fields
sway hello
in time to
that old-time melody
stuck on repeat
I know
the sky must be blue
and the stars
your neighbors
but
I have been
to Paris

THREE GORGES

Soft whiteness
silently enveloping
green blankets
creased with life
hiding
sweat streaked backs
scratched by impatient fingers
breathlessly
escaping dragons
to find heaven's
place of peace

CANCUN

The gulf breeze gently whispers
as triangles dance in the sky
white canopies
earthly escape
hear reborn words with new
faces
tell stories from afar
then jazz tones embrace
and in the warmth
of the mind's womb
silent voices seek mother
listen to returning childhood
echoes
stay true in advice
free in thought
live life beyond breathing
and please find a way
to touch a soul
that will be
your gift
to humanity

Bohemian caravan

In the middle of the desert
who can plan to meet
a cognac sharing man
spirit filled
overflowing
with welcoming love
sharing nights
with free trips to somewhere
journey family
strangers embrace the time
and all give thanks to Val

INCAN MAJESTY

In the land of Juan de Dios
even the heavens cry at such
beauty
drenching tunnels of green
with the music of water
racing to bless
the purple orchards
that ambush the heart
and the yellow leprechauns
that delight the eyes
in whose steps do I follow
along this footworn path of life
to a perfect geometry of stones
a celestial marriage with
Mother Earth

EAGLE ROCK

Like a blind man
I touched the face
but couldn't see it
I did see
the sunlit valley
carpeted in green
yes
that ink blot remains
I'm bound to return
on a different day
compelled to see
that hidden eagle

TAKE A RIDE

On a clear night
before leaving
leave your posse behind
ride deep
go solo
the stars will watch over you
pedal on
you can't get lost
soon you will hear a loud voice
join that conversation
answers awaiting
galactic guidance
to buried questions
you are not alone
traveled tire treads
future companions
know that journey
perhaps a passing star
on its destined journey
finds the light in your darkness
perhaps not
so
with care
listen to the words
coming from your soul
finally
in your very own voice
pedal homeward
burner

Love

ADIEU

When the days of winter
are followed by
the flowers of spring
I think of us
lost in time
compelled to part
like the flitting bee
who flutters
farewell my love
adieu
silence interrupts my lonely
thoughts
as shadows witness
the end of our day

HEALING

The pain of the arrow
stays
deadening that part of you
immunization with a price
straight line living
with no downs
who cares about the ups
don't get close
your friends
are now the arrows
that keep me away
I know
the only way
is to pull each arrow
watch the blood spurt
trickle dry
can you survive the loss
don't look
I will be gentle
but am I
healing you
for someone
else

OUR DAYS

Looking back
I find myself coming to you
still in love
wondering if you remember our
days
today with another
house and two kids
eight-to-five downtown
credit cards and bills
how did that happen
our nights of electric love
days of fun
playing in the soft snow
alone in our world
what a time
how you believed in me
loved me
not seeing then
what I see now
a little too late
would we be different
our love so special
or would we be lost
to the magic of love

As one

At dawn
my pillow
share in sunsets
by my side
with fingers jigsawed together
we speak
silent words
of rainbows and rain
friendly trees
along forgotten paths
that lead nowhere
then a momentary glimpse
of peace on earth
and together
we uncovered
life

WAITING FOR YOU

It may be
too late
when you let go
and want
to try to do
what we needed to do
my heart
is open
my mind wants
to believe
we can do it
I believe
in miracles

ABYSS

If I see the light
could it be life
beyond survival
waiting to reveal
its secret corridor
cobbled and black
yet easy to see
when you close your eyes
blinking in starkness
I saw those scales fixed in balance
immovable the disparate become
partners together forever
and I wondered
where does the pain go

1177

Caressing hands of
mother's
wash clean the souls
of you startled sons
lull them asleep
with your whispering words
of love
kissing their foreheads
as you quietly
murmur your
prayer of peace
then
gently
slip
away

Soul eye

Moonbeams and sun rays
bedfellows
weaving invisible threads
into a tapestry of fate
a beloved birthday gift
ready for the party game
a scavenger hunt
in search of the true dimension
always seeking that invisible key
who will find the secret pathway
whose hidden garden of love
anointed in the light of peace
creates lifetimes from such moments
so impossible in beauty
surely only hallucinating visions
with eager time suspended
but no
earthly eyes can lock
in magical trance
such a heavenly partnership
only the stars can see
with thanks my soul
now in fullness
enjoined

ALL STARS

Detached couples
seemingly involved
in each other's lives
intimately discussing
everything else
till occasion
sees them apart
breathing afresh
at night
walking with stars
a timeless encounter
creates oneness
infinite sacrifice
witnessed by none
how different
from the sun and moon
waltzing apart

Unforgotten

I've been to the forest of could-have-beens
where shafts of sunlight shine their magic
between the silent shaded sentries
of unprotected leaves
naked in death
whispering stories
so real save touch
beyond even earthly happiness
is this the leaf
that speaks to me
in ways only I can know
such colors
even dispossessed
a secret power to be shared
now gently placed by my heart
come
let me wipe your tears
I miss you too

SMITTEN

Treading softly
I smelled some flowers
till I found you
magically enchanting
away from the path
half hidden in the shade
no thorns to frighten
but
is it
too sweet
to last
too new
to be real
are you
just my
in-between lover

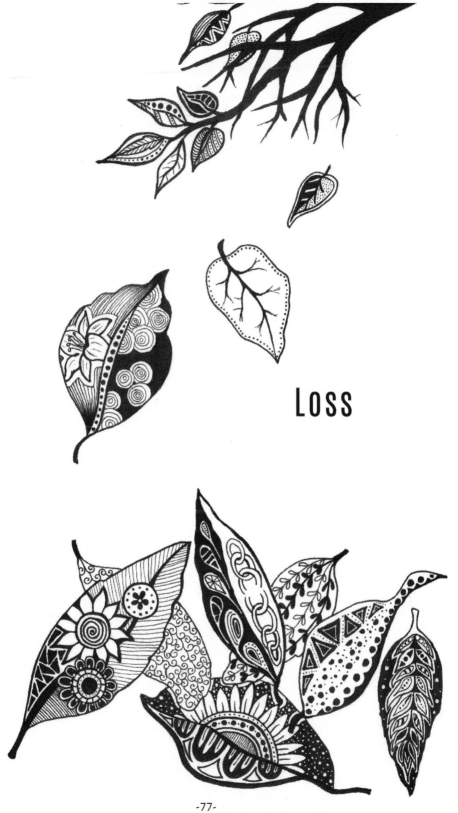

Loss

FALL

Like
fall leaves
we too must separate
remember
those colors
they are inside of you
too

PURPLE FLOWERS

When the weather
returns you to me
and your distant gaze
warms me
I remember that
I am alive
too often I return
to your new home
flowers in hand
the purple ones
you liked so much
now telling you what
I always forgot to share
so the heaviness remains
each day
like turning pages
of some stranger's
faded album
absentmindedly tearing pages
from my daily calendar
I need fixing

GOODNIGHT

Little friend
giving me
all of you
with much love
and innocence
my rock
waiting for your beacon
to fade
as I prepare
to depart
makes our days
endless
with no setting sun
to say goodnight
only shared moments
that stars understand
and we feel
but soon forget
that feeling
and left with a memory
I'll leave
my best friend

FAMILY REBEL

What perfect parent
deserves a single rebel child
so sad to see you lost
my lonely black sheep
destroying yourself
believing in your coat of invincibility
your mind's trick
to steal you from your family
a devil intent
on taking all of me
keep clear
I beg
stay in your cell
leave your innocent siblings in peace
for even sleepless with worry
we will fight back
with bullets you can't see
and words you may hear
but always with prayers
to return us all
to our old family

Soar

I see
my pain
in your eyes
and the words
you don't speak
tell me
you understand
that you see
behind those
handcrafted
clay masks
but take courage
your wings
will soon take you
away
even if we had
to stop right at the end
you aged some
years
but my pride is
to see you and know
that you are
real
and you will do it

The backyard blues

The words I could have said are still inside of me
so I dream of what could have been
and wonder where you are
do you miss my arm in the evening chill
did I ever touch you right

so now that you're out of sight
I just sit around
seeing what I never saw before

didn't my eyes say it all
didn't my smile warm you
did you only hear the words I said
was the silence too lonely for you
couldn't you hear my heart shouting your name

I see your smile in the ripples of my pond
I feel your touch in the midday sun
I miss your words in the shadows of the moon

I heard them all

Unmasked

When I tried to find you
why did you run away
was it a game
or were you
afraid of what I would find
you hid yourself
so well
that I couldn't find you
until I did
one day
by mistake
and saw this was no game
but two faces
and one wasn't
my friend
but which should I trust
the one you see
you said
I chose to believe
silly me

Blurry eyes

Ravishing senses
in a hopeless quest
a goodbye's lingering gaze
creates eternal moments
beyond earthly knowledge
invisible communication
to be savored
sometimes unexpectedly
replacing dreary days
with dreams of reality
till detachment doubts the moment
and distance dulls the taste
forever the saddest word
goodbye

TOO LATE

Buried hearts
lie uncovered
waiting
to share untold stories
only different smiles
for different faces
reveal
a touch of life
locked words
forever secrets
sadly
till only history's friends
can guess the
feelings never said
from stone lips

JAIL TIME

As an escapee on the run
time not done
now sitting silently
with other mourners
in a timber temple of tears
listening to trembling voices
tell their stories
I saw the pictures
heard the howls
embraced some with a healing hug
for who can hide in such light
my aged tears fell slowly
creating volcanoes in the sand
yet still left wondering
could I have done more
to change the path you chose
suddenly alone
left to nurture
the flowers
we lovingly planted
whose colors today blaze brilliantly
head bowed

my blurry eyes questioning
does mourning ever end
to be left to simply miss you
with laughter and dry eyes
patiently awaiting
the official release
from my runaway breakout
in time
for some unknown reason
drawn to look up high
and there
alone on the timbers
scrawled in large bold letters
staring down at me
is your message
I AM FREE

I'LL MISS YOU

I'll never know your story
see you smile
laugh
and cry
nor feel your touch
you'll never have me wipe your tears
hold your hand
hug you tight
we'll never share sunsets
walks in the rain
or have our long afternoons of passion
I'll never have your head on my shoulder
your leg enfolding mine
nor hear the things we'd hoped to say
I'll miss hearing your heart in your voice
those words from your eyes
I'll miss the silence of love
could we have found that magical place
if even for a moment
no more
such a beautiful souvenir
from travels anew
so worth the sadness of goodbyes to
come
and the days keep passing

SHARED HEARTS

I know
your pain
big guy
only now can
I cry
my tears of grief
for my missing dad
and I cry with you
for the loss
that shares our hearts
in love
we have each other
but how I
miss the daily moments
of laughter and
leading you to be you
and now you will
be a different you
try to remember
the dad you once had
such a special bond
I feel my time
with you is
on a timed fuse
ticking to take you
away from
me

NEXIT

Gasping for breath
the mind flooded
with years of tears
a struggle to live
trying so hard to save us both
swimming with just one hand
how long can I keep you afloat
kick your feet
kick your feet
but don't go back there
my words are lost
carried out to sea
the only voice I hear is me
me talking to me
no
me yelling at me
to find terra firma
to survive this unknown cold
tiring arms warning the end is
near
just my spirit left to save me
so
with courage
yesterday's dreams buried
with a serene eulogy
delivered on a beautiful day
surrounded by an ocean
of new dreams

RETURN

I get no message
what am I waiting for
smoke signals
from afar
telling me to stay
the signal will come
the day I turn
my back
returning to my
safe house
love's trick
on life
near misses
and could-have-beens
should-haves
and didn'ts
firm steps
crunch the gravel
telling you
you're alive
the sky is still blue
flowers do bloom
and inside of me
I offer my hand
to me
and find
my best friend

Time

THOSE PEOPLE

New in the job
and eager to please
important to show
mister big
what you can do
add up that
time
and see dollar signs
in the pupil of his eye
good for you
good for him
then let him show you
some fancy tricks
isn't that smart
and It took more
time
ding ding
please meet
counselor ego and
associate ambition
survivors in the big firm
keep the partners happy
is the game
screw the client
is its name

ANOTHER DAY AT THE OFFICE

A meeting was held
and then
another
and after that meeting
another meeting
was followed by
another
meeting
after that
another meeting took place
then
suddenly another
meeting
followed by three
successive meetings
then a meeting was canceled
but quickly
replaced with
another meeting
and then
another

No refund

Give me a refund
it doesn't work
like you advertised
I followed the instructions
kind of
but I did try again
and then it worked
for a while
quite a while
but never properly
it did an okay job
but it wasn't perfect
I could tell
then it started to play up
and I tried to fix it
but it was broken
so now give me a new one
or my money back
because it came
with a
lifetime guarantee

Diagnosis

Stars and stripes
surrounded by wood paneled walls
where history unfolds itself
to the disinterested
and every word
is recorded
for some 21st century
expert who will
clearly understand
what went wrong
with the Land of Liberty
and the People of the Lamp
coining some new buzz words
like
narcissistic materialism
egocentric self-domination
male transfer syndrome
responsible neglect
infectious Hollywood dream disease
maybe even
unintentional family avoidance
but there will be
some rational reason
that it was okay
why
that time
became
the take years

DADDY'S GONE

Moments float by
like clouds drifting
across a blue sky
seemingly not moving
but changing shapes
and shadows tell
a different story
when you
become unhypnotized
yet still frozen
by inaction
you can see
it all
dreaming that a
daddy will take
care of everything
and when tears
find their way out
startled by remembering
the pain of it all
daddy's gone
so you hope yesterday
took care of some problems
till one day
there is no tomorrow
only a final yesterday

WAITING

He's a fat cat
living off me and my work
in at nine
out at three
Thursday it's golf
and August it's Europe
no budget to balance
just a bottomless well
of credit cards and cash
to entertain any fancy
collecting cars like schoolboys
the matchbox series
he says he's earned it
I say he stole it
legally
from me
and people like me
mostly black
like a patronizing grandfather
he tells us
we're lucky
lucky to have work
never mind the pay
is this life

where are my rights
where is my dignity
hidden in some magician's top hat
I'm still waiting to see the main show
and not the second-rate supporting act
can you hear the slow handclap
and the booing
I suppose you can't
it's not for an encore
it's impatience for the main act
but my fat cat boss
can't hear
as he drives by in his
air-conditioned Jag
he'll be home soon
and behind his security gates
he'll sip a scotch in selfish contentment
blissfully unaware
that I'll still be waiting
always waiting
today it's Putco
another breakdown
that's what they always say

Tiger tailed

American voters looking for answers
welcome to my home
I'll take that
thank you
this is all so new
not quite the usual host
get over it
I'm told
confidently waiting for my moment
practiced for this one take
is one ever ready
remember not to be tripped up
by one too many
and now the main event
but first my lines
then sudden panic
she's waiting for me
no mask to prevent airborne confusion
too many faces
who are these wide-eyed people
staring at me

the lights too bright
the heat too hot
I need air
no one is talking
why is no one talking
all eyes fixed on me
African memories return
of headlights
frozen eyes in the night
then back in a flash
now I'm listening to her
familiar faces
slowly return to focus
much to hear
more to learn
in questions answered
only later with relief
to hear my lines
perfectly delivered
be sure to vote
thank you for coming
goodnight

My turn

Rotted dreams
in senility
ripen to illusions
like fruit
beyond welcoming eyes
reality loses its charm with age
and time an orphan
of my history
yields no pity
to weary bones of ex-champions
but I am still here
sadly apologetic
for the need of a giving hand
a smile you can't see
is all that's left to give
even though
I do know you all
oh
that's a mumbled thank you
too

SCARS

Time stopped
for you
a lonely thirteen-year-old
whose year lasted ten
and your pain
became so buried
you couldn't see the scar
some of us could
and one day
you did
what's this
someone tell me
where this came from
will it help
to know
or can that
cosmetic surgeon
smooth it all away
and bring back
feeling
or are those nerves
dead forever
were they ever dead
or was it
self-administered lidocaine
protection from that invisible knife

THEN AND NOW

Protective walls securely hide
what's not to share
naked souls in public confession
even in sunlight
shadows follow
less to be seen
stoic statue
hardly smiling
purposefully pointing away
then
not now
use drapes for new windows
like sunscreen
intelligence your invisible shield
freely smile
just as true rivers flow and tributaries connect
your height in spirit measured
as ambushes abound
with grace
courage is your history

SUNDAY

Say goodnight Sunday
you good for nothing
lazy friend
I'll miss you
must we wait
till next week
you're so busy
who has the time
but you are
the nicest
most boring
and dependable
friend
I'll see you
same time
same place

UNCHANGING ROADS

Where are you going
crossing mountains
draped in a brick shawl
down the silk road
passing Tashkent
to worlds anew
in Viking ships
new horizons
bearded helmets
searching for
some answers
pharaohs found
in monuments of sweat
others in a forty-year walk
discovered one
and later
one became two
for some even three
along cobbled roads

spread like
rivulets of spilled wine
leathered peat
marched in time
to the notes of their turn
roads across seas
became dreams
for roads in the sky
soon built
witnessed by the unbelieving
onward to space
searching for
the secret road of time
in disconnected fashion
a road of sound
of space and glass
instantly connects
yet
still left wondering
if where we came from is
where we are going

LIGHT

In darkness there is light
yet the power to see sleeps
till alarms trigger the mind
even in stark daylight
rushed lives
blindly sleepwalk
ask why nature hides itself
with unseen flowers and invisible trees
lost clouds and forgotten sunsets
too many lost moments
not for you
in life be light
be sure to take your share
and more
for the heavier load
prepares you well
let spirit guide
and your smile unfold
in your daily dance
with time

DAWN'S HAND

Sadness sees no light till dawn
when darting sparrows become homebound
know too
that suckled milk
in bellies
will soon arrive
as petals awakening
slowly stretch
as the hours share their time
think sweetly of golden days
receive the touch of others
trusting hidden wounds do heal
and when visiting that unseen place
less daunting in time
notice how that scar
in it's comforting familiarity
does lose its edge

READY OR NOT

Like a train
whizzing past
we are overtaken
by time

not seeing
not believing
and maybe
not caring
about what's going on
out there

lost in our little worlds
we build cocoons
to reject intruders
with fancy new ideas
so that we may happily
sleepwalk our way
through life

and yet
there are some
like another breed
who seek new horizons
with hidden possibilities
challenging the old with the new

they said it couldn't be done

electric light
men in flight
a voice from the box
acrylic socks

man in space
remodeled face
transplanted hearts
electronic parts

computers galore
calculators and more
a test tube baby
they said maybe

what is to come
it's all been done
the future is coming
are you ready

THE PRICE

What breathless encounter
can own the heart
and lose the mind
vomiting words
desperately denying
not me
yet who can't miss
that puzzle piece
you pray
is never found
safety for sins
fast disappearing
rearview mirrors
goodbye trick
never gone
just hidden
no future
till history arrives

SPACE

The end is never near
time clones itself
into particles of infinity
just find the switch

Death

LEFT

Old man
give up
and die
you've seen it all
done it all
what's left
death
must be
your ultimate experience
so enjoy it
that fleeting moment
of eternity
when pain
becomes a sensual
orgasm of first
experience
and
passing through
that
desert of white light
you will
know that
you have
left

FOREVER THERE

My flag cried
today
its fabric
draped over
crumpled shoulders
of sadness
intact

but my blurry eyes
saw just
one star
and only
two stripes

as brothers traveling
on a family trip
each falling tear
alone
escorting
a dream in a memory
to the dust below

and forever
will that taste
linger
so
even when

my flag again waves
its welcoming arms
and salutes
the unknown
that we all know
today
I may just cry

FALLEN SHADOW

See the day's special in the morning sun
fresh green apples carefully stacked
on a two-wheeled wooden handcart
a father's job no less
ready to sweeten parched mouths
for some loose change
here at the square
where cowardly eyes lurk
searching for innocent prey
a sinister trap
between unseen cross hairs
then tumbling away in slow motion
a carpet of red apples quickly unfurls
on bent knees with loving arms
an unbelieving son embraces his father
sobbing for help that does not come
oh
storied cobblestones
why spread your tears of pain
once more
for us our only prayer
again the same
return soon
the forgotten echoes of laughing children
inshallah

A BROTHER'S FAREWELL

Let the angels pull the arrows from your
heart
let them
love
bathe
and heal you
soon your touch
they too will feel
in the night
I will hear you giggle
hear them laugh
and so will I
if in disbelief
you happen to gaze
upon your goodbye
know the seeds of those flowers
will blow far
carried in the winds of kindness
upon clouds of compassion
for the too soon sick
each a prince
you never met
know you well
not in majesty
but as I did
in truth my words were born
in love shall I honor them
your saplings shall the wind protect
in your shade shall they grow
in time
their towering shadow shall protect
till then carefully shall we
nourish
both roots and shape

so sunshine they can enjoy
and cloudy days endure
freely breathing
life's fresh breeze
tasting the magic of discovery
your heavenly prayer
on Earth
shall we answer
to the boys
I say
I am of you
too soon have you seen
each day's forever grip on life
tomorrows will sadly
bring only fading memories
joyous smiles will return
let pity not distract
as history delivers its untimely challenge
in sadness build strength
in joy proudly carry
the standard of Mummy
with respect
honor your traditions
one day
your standard will alight
and to your flame
others shall follow
be true in action
strong in spirit
for battles yet to face
remember
mothers
will forever thank
your mother

A DIFFERENT DAY

Wearied leather-covered feet
march smooth yon storied cobblestones
in unison follow the murmuring curses
carried in breezes
to reach villager's ears
they come
children cried
yet only the brave
witness sweating manhood
now erect with swift steps
in search of destiny
where fresh lands beckoned
sadly no glamorous end
for history to record
mostly rotting bodies of the unknown
save the sorry survivors
blamed for breathing
the air of their fallen brethren
so different to the air of the victors
now fresh with invisible spirit
lifting wearied warriors
to fly with the clouds
and sing with the moon

THE LEFT BEHINDS

Which bridge high enough
to end this day in full sun
a perilous climb to a simple fall
racing with gravity
the goal clear
that blue line crossed in solo victory
no cheering crowds in your lonely triumph
left wondering what game the mind played
the pictures you might have seen
the thoughts you could not share
with the loving left behinds

MY DASH

Bff ily
my little body has room for nothing else
stay young
dear friends
losing memory
a bad habit of age
hold tight that locket of our times
that will be me
touching your heart
with a sudden jolt of joy
nothing is forgotten
sorries pleases thankyous unsaid
words with unborn feelings
everything is remembered
like that deep explosion
from the belly of a volcano
how we laughed
or if ever we cried
our tears could fill oceans
I see it all in a flash now
shots and braces
carpools and classrooms
vacations and places
and the faces
so many faces

along that never-ending path
twisting with magical surprises
barely stopping
I always drank long
from the cup of my teachers
living to learn
or is it the other way
best listen well in that class
so for pure love
free to touch and be touched
thank you
stay well
clutch that locket sometimes
and think of me on another road
that dash on my stone
is all of you

THE DINNER SERVICE

Survivors
of love and disdain
of utility and beauty
whose day may end
with a sudden crash
surrounded by tears and apologies
hushed whispers in dark corners
by the others left behind
wondering
where are you
till the stack finally accepts
you are not lost
but gone
yet what of the cracked ones
guilty survivors of attachment
such unique care
for what is truly broken
flaws in hiding
waiting for a slip and a fall
or maybe a new housekeeper
sweeping clean
the old
the broken
the not so pretty

suddenly in breathless panic
left to wonder
where are those familiar hands I know so well
what news of the others in my stack
and the rest of the drawer
relief
I hear you say
the end of special care
the end of pity
the end of shame
they will remember you
some may miss you
but your turn is sadly done
time to make space for the new
so make peace with dinners past
before your final give
and proudly share
your cracked smile
with a grateful finger wave

GETTING THERE

Everything is in silence
the angels have no voice
waiting for the chosen to
signal their time of escape
then to be lifted with ease
in a suspended journey
to someplace else
where sight is unseen
with no touch
in unknown union
an elevated dimension
not imaginable
but first the journey
destined to be so different
for the worst
the best
and the in-betweens
finally
for all
the same destination

NORMANDY

No stories from the silenced dead
less from
the living
just love for buddies
resting in the grass
companions forever
and
ein deutscher Soldat
now a friendly neighbor
reminding the visitor
on the day that end began
when the sea ran red
the young died old
and
freedom's bloody foothold
assured the death of evil
so many lifetimes lived in a day
now forever that day
a free world
etched on marble pillows
every soldier's
living legacy
for nobody dies at eighteen

Spirit

GOT RELIGION

I believe
just not like you
not as much
even differently
do you believe
too much
maybe
I don't believe
enough

DREAM ON

Hunting dreams
no sport of the young
untethered in flight
touching clouds in wonderment
unearthly senses
see no boundaries
the night heavens
pathways to fulfillment
dream on
my children
let not the weariness of age
corrupt the beauty of hope
nor dull the light of discovery
dream on
forever children
with spirits filled we can remain

A TALE

Fortune smiles upon
unmet creatures of the Universe
travelling from galaxies afar
in unknown space
that suddenly collide
in brilliance
creating new light
from a fusion of differences
now in harmony speeding
beyond mortal sight to
a celestial home of giving
in peace and wonderment
like the mermaid
and the pirate
of ancient lore

FOREVERLAND

When touch
fails to warm
who can blame
the withered remnants of a heart
rebirthing in some silk-lined
steel encased
tomb
immunity
finally
from hot hands
with capturing smiles
and untrue breath
in the scent of seasons
roses in bloom
let hearts escape
to suddenly pulsate
swaggering in omnipresence
like a butterfly
unprotected
again
to believe in forever

A PRAYER

Before my dust falls to the wishes of the winds
before my spirit settles in your bosom
before judgment of my earthly days
let me walk in the garden of peace
give me strength to be better
give me the will to act
give me the insight to know your path
let me honor you as a man of God

Rebirth

Salted words
from the heart
streak across the face of life
in a galactic journey
into a darkness
blindly careening
in a tunnel of black confusion
breathless in panic
till time fractionates
returning sight for the unseeing
a kaleidoscopic symmetry
expanding and slowing
the black hole
and new vision sees
overcome by calmness
in control
when light as we know it
starkly etched
by recognizable objects
enters a familiar world
with strange sensation
of rebirth
signaling the end of
God's prayer

CELESTIAL FAMILY

My ancestors thought of me today
that sacredness
is the beauty
of my own gift
to that piece of civilization's future
there is no final realization
no happily ever after
just a single step
in the work of who you are not
reimagining your place
on Mother Earth
finding connectedness
not to humans
rather to the non-humans
never isolated in a bigger family
more than just being human
a unique earthborn cell
in a face of mystery
in awe of all chosen
a holy spinning planet
of infinite wonder
with possibilities beyond dreams
touching your nakedness
in a kiss of peace
till
your
very
last
breath

THREE QUESTIONS

I LOVE

Did I love enough
in time
will be the first question
with calm breath and tight fist
be ready to say
yes
for always let your energy
flow like ripples
creating circles of love
embracing all around
your simple smile beckoning
open arms enfolding
perhaps your eyes
a lighthouse
on some other's journey
your giving light
creating the natural beauty
of pure love
feel it all

II RECEIVE

Was I loved enough
shall follow
this second question
such a tortuous memory maze
eternal moments
of time and space
of people and places
so too along your journey
learn how to receive
that untaught art of embracing
another's aura of giving
a secret too late uncovered by many
forget fast those taking skills
where greed attractively costumed
hides the insecurity of naked wants
return to yourself
and be forever grateful
for all of the love

III FORGIVE

Is there anything left unsaid
the final question to answer
before the galactic gates
welcome you to the cosmos
with little thought
in your last breath
the answer shall be no
for love will find the right words
so trust your heart
let your eyes speak their truth
know that good thoughts may never be
said
nor telegraphed to those on your mind
because the burden of words
is yours to carry
so with clarity of voice
share the feelings in dark shadows
and remember the path to peace
forgive and be free

IV ACT

So now
with thanks
go forth
your journey continues
smile joyfully
with an open heart
gentle words and strong spirit
freely love
receive
forgive
each day
ready
in the here and now
to touch and be touched

ACKNOWLEDGMENTS

Someone once reflected that I must have been loved by many people when I was growing up. For as long as I can remember, I have always been blessed to be surrounded by so much love. Thanks to that ever-present love, I developed a strong sense of identity, internal peace, and confidence for which I am grateful.

Nevertheless, I have not been immune to the failings of the human condition. I have also felt loss and disappointment. I have experienced betrayal and confusion. Yet, I hold no grudges and carry no regrets. Instead, I choose to be forgiving and resilient.

I owe so much to the communities that have supported me over the years; they have all served me well, just as I did my best to serve them. Metal International, Burning Man, The OK Corral are some recent examples of communities that have encouraged my growth and evolution. The individuals within those communities have brought inspiration, excitement, challenges, and magic to my journey of life.

Special thanks to those of you who picked me up when I was down and helped me return to my magnetic north. To those who opened my eyes, I thank you for helping me see. To the loves of my life, I offer a knowing embrace. For all the others who have crossed my path, I send warm hugs and well wishes. As for the strangers I long to meet, I look forward to that future delight.

To KE, who midwifed this book of poems, your insight and assistance has been invaluable in bringing this creation into form.

To my children, David, Tracy, Daniel, Nathaniel, and Erin, all I can say is that I searched for the right words in the dictionary. They are just not there.

To all of my grandchildren, cousins, aunts, uncles, close friends, and mentors, to be as
inclusive as possible, I will acknowledge each of you by listing the first letter of your first name:
QWERTYUIOPASDFGHJKLZXCVBNM.
I appreciate and love you all.

I also give thanks to Mother Earth, the Stars, the Moon and the Sun for their inspiring
presence.

Finally, I wish to acknowledge my mother Mathilde Gordon—known and loved throughout the world. Last year, on her 100th Birthday, the only gift I could come up with was a card thanking her for all of the knowledge she'd imparted to me over the years. I leave you with just one of those
lessons, "No matter how good you are, there is always room for improvement."

Made in the USA
San Bernardino, CA
29 April 2020